# ENGAGING TEACHING TOOLS

## Measuring and Improving Student Engagement

**David Sladkey**

**FOR INFORMATION:**

Corwin
A SAGE Company
2455 Teller Road
Thousand Oaks, California 91320
(800) 233-9936
www.corwin.com

SAGE Publications Ltd.
1 Oliver's Yard
55 City Road
London EC1Y 1SP
United Kingdom

SAGE Publications India Pvt. Ltd.
B 1/I 1 Mohan Cooperative Industrial Area
Mathura Road, New Delhi 110 044
India

SAGE Publications Asia-Pacific Pte. Ltd.
3 Church Street
#10-04 Samsung Hub
Singapore 049483

Acquisitions Editor: Jessica Allan
Cover Designer: Anupama Krishnan
Typesetter: C&M Digitals (P) Ltd

Copyright © 2014 by David Sladkey

All rights reserved. When forms and sample documents are included, their use is authorized only by educators, local school sites, and/or noncommercial or nonprofit entities that have purchased the book. Except for that usage, no part of this book may be reproduced or utilized in any form or by any means, electronic or mechanical, including photocopying, recording, or by any information storage and retrieval system, without permission in writing from the publisher.

Printed in the United States of America

*A catalog record of this book is available from the Library of Congress.*

ISBN 978-1-4833-1641-3

This book is printed on acid-free paper.

14 15 16 17 18 10 9 8 7 6 5 4 3 2 1

# About the Author

**David Sladkey** has been teaching high school mathematics since 1987. He was named Teacher of the Year for Naperville Community School District 203 in 2007 and the Office Max Innovative Teacher of the Month in March of 2009. David is the author of *Energizing Brain Breaks*, a Corwin bestseller. The book includes 50 fun challenges for brain and body to help you and your students regain focus. David loves to get his students moving and participating actively in their learning. He appreciates technology that impacts curriculum and is easy to implement. David uses a

SMART Board in his classes every day and is the mathematics department technology specialist. He has co-authored a book, "Easy SMARTBoard Teaching Templates," with Scott Miller. David is passionate about his teaching and reflects this journey in his blog Reflections of a High School Math Teacher (teachhighschoolmath.blogspot.com). David is also an avid cyclist and loves spending time with his wife and three children.

"The great aim of education is not knowledge, but action."

Herbert Spencer
1820–1903

# Welcome to **Engaging Teaching Tools**

Students want to be involved in their learning. They are eager to be active and engaged. This little flip book will give you a way to check the engagement level of your students. It will also give you 50 practical, ready to use teaching ideas.

- The first part of the book helps you measure student involvement with a self evaluation tool called the Engagement Wheel. The Wheel can also guide your lesson planning to incorporate engaging activities.

- The second part of the book deals with different strategies to help promote your classroom's engagement; these include Questioning, Classroom Climate, Classroom Aids, Attitude Adjustment, and Parents.

By experimenting with the ideas in this book, you will find your teaching refreshed and your classroom more inviting. I hope you enjoy reading **Engaging Teaching Tools** in short time increments. It is a compilation of my own ideas as well as those of many other teachers in their classroom experiences. Some have already been suggested by other authors and will be cited as much as possible.

Additional materials and resources related to *Engaging Teaching Tools* can be found at www.corwin.com/teachingtools.

Enjoy! David Sladkey, dsladkey@gmail.com

# Table of Contents

## Engagement Wheel
1. Student Engagement Wheel
6. Have a Student Teach the Class Something
7. Partner/Group Work
8. Hands-On Technologies
9. Hands-On Activities
10. Choosing Students at Random
11. Make Your Students Laugh Out Loud
12. Make Time for Self-Reflection
13. Movement in Class
14. Show Your Students a Media Clip
15. Let Students Give Their Opinion

## Questioning
17. Reverse Your Questions
18. Expect 100% Participation in all Class Activities.
19. Answer Questions in a Variety of Ways
20. Pause
21. "I Don't Know" Doesn't Fly
22. Stop Finishing Your Students' Sentences
23. Think Before You Use Sarcasm
24. Stop and Ask "What Comes Next?"

## Classroom Climate
26. Greet Each Student Personally Everyday
27. Make a New Seating Chart Every 3 Weeks
28. Notice When a Student Is Absent
29. Admit Your Mistakes
30. Guest Introductions
31. Take ACTion
32. Private Discipline
33. New Partner "Get to Know You" Questions
34. Picking Roles in Partner/Group Work

## Classroom Activities

36 Importance Order
38 Circuits
40 Auditory Sentence Ordering
42 Easy Video Recorders
44 Left-Right Talking (Structured Partner Work)
45 Energizing Brain Breaks
46 Take a STAND

## Classroom Aids

48 Invest in a Timer
49 Music During Assessments and Work Time
50 Communicating With Your Students at Eye Level
51 Circular Teacher's Desk
52 Partner Desk Set-Up
53 Fidgety Students
54 Personal Mini White Boards

## Attitude Adjustment

56 Don't Complain...Teach Them!
57 Name 13 Virtues of a Teacher
58 20 Years Later
59 Every Student Has a Story
60 Name Five Things You Are Grateful For
61 Reflect on Each One of Your Students

## Parents

63 Power of the Parent
64 Open Parent/Guardian Communications Early
65 Invite Parents/Guardians to Visit the Class

## Extras

67 Book Discussion Questions
68 References
69 Acknowledgments

vii

# ENGAGEMENT WHEEL

# Student Engagement Wheel

## The Student Engagement Wheel measures student involvement.

The Student Engagement Wheel is a self-assessment tool for teachers to check the engagement level of their students. The Wheel has ten spokes. Each spoke represents a different way in which you can get your students engaged in the lesson. If you use the Wheel before your lesson, you can scan the areas on the spokes of the Wheel to see which ones you hope to accomplish. If you are reflecting after a lesson, you can actually measure class engagement level numerically. The number is determined by the number of spokes that you have accomplished in that lesson. For instance, if your class participated in a partner or group activity, then you could count that spoke. Add up all the spokes that are true for that class period and you would have an idea of the engagement level for your students. Ideally you would get an average score for the same class measured over an entire week.

# HOW TO USE THE ENGAGEMENT WHEEL

1. Choose a class period that you have recently completed. It could be just a one-hour segment of your day to reflect on.

2. Count the total number of spokes (pie pieces) that are true for that class period to determine your student's engagement level.

3. Do this over a number of days and determine an average engagement level for your class.

| Total Number of Filled in Pie Pieces | Student Engagement Level |
|---|---|
| 0–1 | LOW |
| 2–3 | |
| 4–5 | |
| 6 and up | HIGH |

A student taught/explained something to the class, a partner, or a small group. **A**

The class spent part of the hour in partner/group activities. **B**

Students used hands-on technology to enhance their learning. **C**

The class performed a lab or hands-on activity for part of the hour. **D**

Students were called on randomly instead of voluntarily throughout the class. **E**

Students laughed out loud at something appropriate in class. **F**

The class was given time to self-reflect during the hour. **G**

Students were out of their chairs for at least one activity during the class. **H**

Students were presented a media clip (video, audio, Internet, newspaper, etc.). **I**

Students gave their opinion on a topic in a group or whole-class setting. **J**

3

Color or B/W
Engagement
Wheel
PDF Masters
are available.

Type the exact web address below to access the PDFs.

http://tinyurl.com/ETIpdfs

Student Engagement Wheel (For Teachers to Self-Assess)

# Example of the ENGAGEMENT WHEEL
## PDF Masters in use

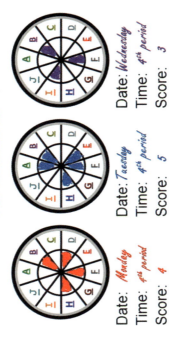

Date: Monday
Time: 4th period
Score: 4

Date: Tuesday
Time: 4th period
Score: 5

Date: Wednesday
Time: 4th period
Score: 3

## Self-Reflections

It was a good week. The class loved the hands-on activity from Monday. I was consistent in having the class work in partner/group activities. I forgot to give my students a Brain Break on Wednesday. I need to call on my students randomly on a regular basis.

# Have a Student Teach the Class Something

## Engagement Wheel Slice "A"

When you teach something, you have to know the material. When you know the material, you will be able to use it. As teachers we sometimes get that good feeling when we have just helped the class to understand something. We should try to get our students to get this same good feeling when they explain something to each other. Students start to "buy in" and "own it" when they teach their classmates a topic. This is called student engagement. We can do this by designing activities that students can work on with a partner or small group. We can also try to find ways to have our students explain things to the whole class. We should think of ourselves as facilitators. My motto is "Let my students teach/explain it."

A student taught/explained something to the class, a partner, or a small group.

A

# Partner/Group Work

### Engagement Wheel Slice "B"

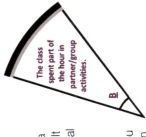

The class spent part of the hour in partner/group activities.

B

Students love to work in a small group setting with a purpose in mind. Small group time is a great way to break up the class period. Small groups give students a voice that they might not use in the large class setting. It allows students to question things that might seem trivial in the larger group setting. Small groups give students confidence when giving their answer to the rest of the class. Partner/Group work does not have to be for a continuous period of time. As a matter of fact, when you vary the group work with other modes of teaching it can be very effective. For example, you could give a problem to the class and have a set time limit for group work. Then have them share their group's findings with the class. This presents a very interactive and engaging class.

# Hands-On Technologies

## Engagement Wheel Slice "C"

Students used hands-on technology to enhance their learning.

C

Calculators, readers, video recorders, audio recorders, phones, tablet computers, hand-held clickers, iPods, iPads, organizers, microscopes, cameras, probes, netbooks, scanners, laptops, GPSs, keyboards, lasers, sonar, and telescopes are all educational resources.

- Stations are excellent uses of Hands-On Technologies.
- Design your activity with content as the end result and the technology as a vehicle to get there.
- Waiting until you are comfortable with a technology might mean NEVER using it in the classroom.
- Consider students' learning curve when choosing a technology.
- Novelty wears out with technology. Don't use a technology unless it helps you master content.

# Hands-On Activities

### Engagement Wheel Slice "D"

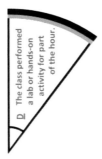

D  The class performed a lab or hands-on activity for part of the hour.

When students participate in a hands-on activity in your class they are more apt to remember the content that goes along with it. Just yesterday in my class a student told his partner, "Remember when we did that activity with the tape and string and we learned about the ellipse?" I was so pleased that he had related his learning back to the activity. We place our students in win-win situations with hands-on activities. First of all, students like the change of pace that goes along with hands-on activities. Secondly, students have something concrete to help them remember the content.
Here are some examples of hands-on activities:
cutting, pasting, measuring, drawing, building, lab work, timing, folding, throwing, catching, moving, binding, constructing, and any hand-held technology.

# Choosing Students at Random

### Engagement Wheel Slice "E"

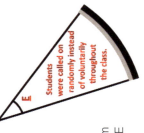

Students were called on randomly instead of voluntarily throughout the class.

Do you want more accountability in your classroom? Select students to answer questions and perform tasks on a RANDOM BASIS. This promotes a safe and fair playing field for all class members. Students like to know that everyone is part of the activities of the class. When you randomly select students for activities, they draw comfort in this. It does make them more accountable because they know they could be called on at any time. When there is a task to perform like an in-class responsibility, then I will choose randomly to select a student.

What is the message that you are conveying with random selection? Fairness! You are telling your class EVERYONE is expected to participate in this class. With a high participation rate, we have a high engagement rate.

# Make Your Students Laugh Out Loud

## Engagement Wheel Slice "F"

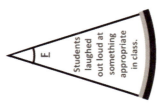

You should try to make your students laugh out loud daily. Laughter breaks tension and encourages engagement. When students are laughing, they are more apt to look forward to your class and ultimately they will want to please you. This is important in discipline. Here are some ideas:

Rotate students to be in charge of a pre-screened daily joke.

Find funny short video clips and show them between activities.

Tell your own funny stories from your past.

Have your students work with a partner and have a "Make your partner laugh" session and then switch roles.

Tell a daily joke or a daily riddle.

# Make Time for Self-Reflection

### Engagement Wheel Slice "G"

Self-reflection is where a student is given time to "think" about how something relates to them. Everyone loves to think and talk about themselves, especially when it is in a structured safe environment. We rarely do this in class because it takes some time. Self-Reflection is a great transition exercise.

1. Give the students some alone time to self-reflect, that is, "You have one minute to reflect."
2. Have them write about their level of confidence in mastering the targets of a unit prior to a test.
3. Give the students a vehicle to express their self-reflection thoughts such as a class discussion, a journal, or a small group setting.
4. Set some time aside for goal setting.

The class was given time to self-reflect during the hour.

# Movement in Class

## Engagement Wheel Slice "H"

We have a tendency to think that quiet seat work equals learning. We have to get over this and start thinking how to design the classroom so the students can MOVE AND LEARN at the same time. When students are moving with a purpose in your classroom, they will be more engaged with what you are doing because they like varied activities. I have given a few strategies in this book like Circuits, Take a Stand, and Energizing Brain Breaks. Here is another example. Passing out Papers: Have a student throw your handout papers up in the air in the front of the room and then have the class go get a paper. Don't ever pass papers out by rows again. Even if you have your students simply stand and stretch, you will be doing their brains a favor.

Students were out of their chairs for at least one activity during the class. **H**

# Show Your Students a Media Clip

## Engagement Wheel Slice "I"

A timely media clip can go a long way in a class to keep students engaged in the topic. A clip can affirm the content that you are trying to get across, especially if it has a funny or bizarre aspect to it. Students will identify with the clip and therefore relate it to the content. For instance if while you are teaching the quadratic formula you take a break and show an Internet clip of someone singing a song to it, then students will tie the content to the song.

Students especially like media clips when they

are in them. Try to find these clips or have your students make them. This is a great way to build your positive classroom climate.

# Let Students Give Their Opinion

## Engagement Wheel Slice "J"

Getting students to participate will increase your student engagement. Polling your students will help your participation level. When students are asked their opinion on a topic, they relate better than if they are just presented the content. A poll that is given without peer pressure is the best type to give. When students have the pressure of giving a certain answer in front of their classmates, they sometimes don't answer honestly. I suggest a clicker hand-held technology device to give a poll. Electronic clickers wirelessly give data to your computer with the results of a question.

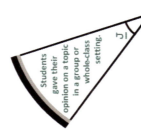

Students gave their opinion on a topic in a group or whole-class setting.

J

These give the students privacy with immediate anonymous results. I like using the clickers because I can vary from the immediate content very easily and go with the flow of the class' opinions.

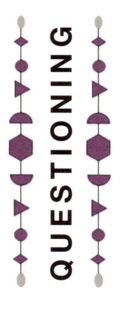
# QUESTIONING

# Reverse Your Questions

Let's say you typically ask this type of question: "Name four states that are on the East Coast." Try this question: "What do New York, Florida, Maine, and New Jersey have in common?" What you are doing is using the answer to the original question as the new question. When you reverse the question, students will have to think about the same topic in a new way. It will stretch their thinking. Here is another example: "What is the verb in this sentence?" Try reversing the question to be, "Here is a verb. What would be an appropriate sentence to use it in?" Almost any question can be reversed. Asking the question in the reverse order not only repeats the idea, but repeats it in a way that is more engaging than the same question over and over. For example,

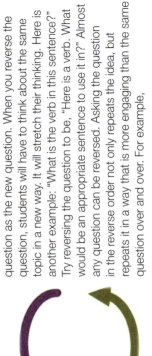

"What is the answer to ½ + ¾?" The reverse of that question is, "Name two fractions that add up to be 1 ¼."

## Expect 100% Participation in All Class Activities

When we do not require all students to participate in a class activity we are sending a subtle message that there are different rules for different students. A student who is allowed to exclude himself from a graded or non-graded activity becomes a cancer in the class and everyone is affected. Here are a couple of ideas to help you strive for 100% participation.

(1) Pick your students to answer questions randomly. This can be done by simply having all the names of your students on separate note cards or craft sticks. When you ask a question, you just pick a card from the deck or a craft stick with a name on it. (2) Communicate your expectations from day one that everyone will participate in every activity. (3) Constant monitoring of what students are actually doing will help you get 100% participation. You can do this by walking around and behind every student. This also helps define your ownership of the classroom space.

# Answer Questions in a Variety of Ways

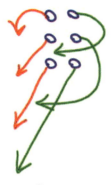

A few years ago, a fellow coach was verbally explaining a soccer drill to me. He went into great detail about how the drill should be done using only words. I did not understand the drill at all and asked him to explain it again. Instead of repeating the same words again, he then got out a piece of paper and wrote the drill out with diagrams. I then completely understood the drill, and I still have the piece of paper today. Our students need the same treatment in our classes. We have to address their misunderstandings in different modes of learning. If the fellow coach continued to repeat the directions verbally, I certainly would not have understood the drill as well. Change your mode of communication with a student who does not understand something. Some possible modes to use may include: visual, auditory, kinesthetic, diagram, chart, map, speech, book, drama, picture, movement, manipulative, video, story, or parable. Resist the temptation to give up. Students will get it. Keep trying new modes.

## Pause

Pausing for someone or something is a sign of respect. We pause for emergency vehicles when they are passing on the road. We pause during a moment of silence. You would pause at the passing of a historic figure.

First, we need to pause before we deliver a message to our students so that everyone will give you their full attention. Ask for their attention and then pause. Don't be afraid to be silent and wait. It might take a while at first. Don't speak until EVERYONE has given you their attention, typically 3–7 seconds. When you start this it might take longer. Pausing also reinforces that there is a transition time.

**3 – 7 seconds**

Now, there is a catch with this type of classroom management. Every time you ask your students to pause, you need to say something important. If you say something trivial every time you ask them to pause, they probably will be less ready to pause for you.

# "I Don't Know" Doesn't Fly

First of all, always give your students "think" time when posing a question. Then, when you have given the right amount of time for the appropriate question, you can pick a student to answer the question. This means the "I don't know" answer may apply, but will not get them out of answering the question. If a student says, "I don't know," then I give them these choices.

**Could I ask a friend for a hint?**

1. You can ask a friend to give you a hint.

2. You can ask a friend to step you through the problem.

3. You can poll the class. For instance, "How many of you think the answer is choice A?"

4. You can ask the teacher to give you a hint.

This type of questioning builds accountability. They know that if they are called, then they will need to answer the question eventually. This helps their mind set when initially working through the question.

# Stop Finishing Your Students' Sentences

A book called *Teach Like a Champion* by Doug Lemov has helped my questioning techniques. My problem was that I praised a student for giving me part of an answer to my question and then I promptly completed their sentence with the correct finished product. Unfortunately, I was robbing them of the opportunity to get it straight in their minds. Students would simply give me something remotely correct, and then I would fill in the rest. My students were turning their minds off after they gave me a small nugget of correct information. Now, I stick with the student until THEY finish it correctly. This takes some time. It is even difficult on the student at times. However, the rest of the class will pick up on this and raise their level of

**Good start. Now you can finish the answer off for us.**

answers. Instead of students giving us a partial answer, they begin to understand the whole answer is needed. You might have to give the student some prompts to be able to finish the answer or use wait time to allow her to think. But ultimately have the student finish her own sentence.

# Think Before You Use Sarcasm

Sarcasm is very funny. However, not all students understand sarcasm and this creates fear. Fear in our classrooms is an enemy to student engagement. Sarcasm is an excuse for some in your class to shut down and not participate verbally. Here is an example. I had a student who day after day did not have her homework. Then, she asked me to repeat the assignment that I had just told the class. I sarcastically said, "I don't need to tell you the assignment because you won't do it anyway." I was trying to communicate a message to her. However, it was at the expense of raising the fear level in my class. I should have communicated my message at another time. I ended up apologizing to her. It was then that I realized the negative power of sarcasm.

ASK YOURSELF THESE QUESTIONS BEFORE YOU USE SARCASM:

1. Is my comment at the cost of a student?

2. Do I need to use sarcasm in this instance?

3. Can I communicate my message in a more dignified manner?

## Stop and Ask "What Comes Next?"

When we get rolling as a teacher, we often lose our students. This is a technique to help keep your students a part of the discussion by asking, "What comes next?" This question creates anticipation and engagement. Students will participate with you and think about what will come next. Here is an example. You are showing a video and you pause it at an appropriate time and ask, "What comes next?" Have them discuss it with a partner for 30-60 seconds and then go back to the video. Another example would be when you are giving a definition to a vocabulary word. You stop in mid-sentence and ask, "What comes next?" This helps students build on what has been stated already and then extend it to what might be covered.

If we give our students opportunities to try to foreshadow what is coming next, we will have students that are engaged in their own learning.

# CLASSROOM CLIMATE

# Greet Each Student Personally Everyday

I heard a piece of coaching advice to try to communicate with EVERY player on your team EACH day. I have translated this idea to the classroom. I now try to greet each one of my students personally every day. It might be at the beginning of the class or somewhere during the class, but I try to communicate with each student each day. Students have the perception that we have favorites. Greeting each student takes that perception away. Also, it takes a little fear out of communicating with us. If a student knows that we have acknowledged them, they are more apt to ask a content-based question of us. The easiest way to do this is to greet them at the door. Another way would be to structure an activity that enables you to bounce from student to student until you have reached everyone. I have to admit, some

students don't always give you the nice smile back. Don't get discouraged, and don't give up. It is well worth the effort. You will see results immediately.

# Make a New Seating Chart Every 3 Weeks

Seating Charts help students feel safe. Students are assigned to a seat and they know they belong there. This is most comforting for the shy students. Change your seating chart every three weeks. When you change your seating chart, have the students do a "get to know you" activity with the people around them. This helps them to start communicating BEFORE they start talking about the material of the class. Changing your seating chart keeps students on their toes and helps prevent bad habits from forming.

Here is an easy way to create a seating chart. Make a card for each student. Place your cards on the desk randomly to make the shape of your classroom desks.

Note: I don't believe in specifically placing high level students with low level students because their processing speed usually differs. Both students seem to get frustrated with this.

# Notice When a Student Is Absent

Whenever students have been absent, take the time to welcome them back and say that you missed them. It seems like a small thing, but it really makes a difference. Just consider how you could impact a student by simply noticing her when she has returned. Maybe you will be the only one at school who notices. It would really help the climate of your classroom and your school if all students knew they were cared for in this one small way.

**We Missed You!**

Here are some things you could say:

1. We missed you.
2. Welcome back.
3. It wasn't the same around here without you.
4. I hope all is well; can I help you get caught up with anything?

Thanks to Pat Quinn who gave me this awesome tip.

# Admit Your Mistakes

It is not easy to admit you are wrong. It takes courage and transparency. It makes you very vulnerable as well. However, when we do admit our mistakes, it creates a respect from our students. Here is an example: I gave a definition of a vocabulary word incorrectly. (I'm embarrassed to say this has happened more than once.) I simply had to own up to it the next day, correct it and tell them that I was very sorry about the mistake. Another example is when I have publicly embarrassed a student. This is also something that I must take responsibility for and ask my class's and the student's forgiveness.

The best thing to do is admit your mistakes before you make them. Ask your students to forgive you for the errors that you will make with them. Ask them to be very watchful to help you catch mistakes. Be real with your students. Be genuine. When you admit your own mistakes, you can bet that your students will be more willing to admit their mistakes.

# Guest Introductions

Whenever you have a guest in the room, it is good to introduce him and also have your students introduce themselves. This acknowledges your guest and connects him to your students. It also helps your students to think outside themselves. Guest introductions are an easy and quick activity.

1. Remind your students to face their guest when they are talking.

2. Students should take turns introducing themselves.

3. Students should say their first name and then answer one simple question that has been posed to the class. Try to have questions that don't have big answers. Here are a couple of examples:

   a. What is an activity/interest that you are involved in?

   b. What is your favorite item for Thanksgiving dinner?

   c. What is your favorite . . . candy . . . color . . . animal?

4. Have your guest introduce himself and answer the question as well. Have him explain why he is there.

# Take ACTion

Students often do things that irritate us. These things can be small actions that are not really against the rules, but they really bug us. It is important for us, as teachers, to deal with these irritations with some type of action. If we don't take action, then things build up and we often explode or do something we shouldn't. The trick is to take action in an honest and tactful way. ACKNOWLEDGE that

there is a problem to the student. Be CONSIDERATE and respectful when working with your student. Act quickly in a TIMELY manner. Taking ACTion could mean a number of things. It could mean simply talking with the student and explaining how we are seeing the situation and asking for help in resolving the issue. It could also mean

**A** cknowledge
**C** onsiderate
**T** imely

communicating with the parents, school counselor, nurse, or psychologist. Finally, it could mean giving out consequences, remembering that you should always give small consequences to start and gradually increase the penalties.

# Private Discipline

Everyone likes to be treated with dignity. Our students deserve to be respected at all times, even when we are disciplining them. When an issue comes up in class, try to first discreetly communicate your intentions. If this doesn't work, then ask that the student see you after class for a discussion about the incident. There are many reasons for you to do this.

**Please see me after class.**

1. You and the student will get some "think" time on the incident.

2. Other students are not influencing the discipline process. Most students need an audience to act out.

3. This process shows we care about the student.

4. This process allows other issues to be discussed. This is a good time to "listen" to some possible things that are underlying issues for the student.

# New Partner "Get to Know You" Questions

**I'd like to introduce Kelly, and the state she would like to go to is Alaska.**

When students are working in a new group or when you change the seating chart, you should have some "get to know you" interview questions. This is something very easy to do, and the students really enjoy it. The purpose is to begin dialogue between students *before* content based material is covered. This effectively puts each student on the same playing field. First pair up your students whenever you create a new seating chart or create new groups. Second, give them 3–4 "get to know you" questions, with time to talk about them. Third, share aloud by having your students introduce their partner and answer one of the questions.

Sample Questions: What are some interests or activities that you are involved in? What pets do you have and what are their names? Name your top three fast food restaurants? Which state do you most want to go to but haven't been there yet?

# Picking Roles in Partner/Group Work

If your students are doing partner/group work, then there needs to be designated roles such as a reader, a scribe, or someone to pick up materials. To choose this person, suggest a list of random factoids your students can use to figure out who has the role in the group. This builds community and the students like it. Here are some samples:

- the person who has the most siblings

- the person whose first name is the longest

- the person who most recently ate a _____ (hot dog, orange, etc.)

- the person who is closest to the _____ (flag, door, stapler, etc.)

- the person whose _____ of birth is largest (day, month)

- the person whose handspan is largest (stretched thumb to pinky)

- the person who most recently watched a movie

- the person who lives the farthest from school

# CLASSROOM ACTIVITIES

# Importance Order

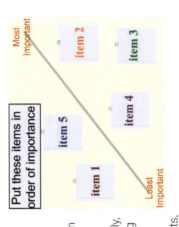

A great way to engage your students is to give them an opportunity to share their opinion. The idea of Importance Order is to give a list of 5–10 items to your students and have them order them from most important to least important. This activity usually generates a lot of discussion and passion. Most importantly, the dialogue between students is dealing with the content that you want them to know! Here are some ideas for items to list: characters in a book, historical events, class behaviors, or methods/steps of solving a problem. This activity works great with an interactive white board.

# DIRECTIONS FOR IMPORTANCE ORDER

1. Draw a large 4-foot diagonal line on your front board. Write "Most Important" at the top of the diagonal line and write "Least Important" at the bottom of the diagonal line.

2. Write your 5–10 items on separate pieces of paper that can be seen from any location in the room.

3. Tape them to the front board around the diagonal line in random order.

4. Give the class time to work in pairs and discuss their order. Partners have to agree on an order.

5. Randomly call up pairs to place any one item where they think it belongs. They must justify why they think it belongs there.

6. Repeat step 5 until all the items are placed on the line. Allow other groups to move items that were previously set. Always ask students to justify their work.

# Circuits

Do you want a great break from the traditional worksheet? Circuits are stations around the room where students work on problems or an activity. Circuits help students move and learn and remember the problems they did at certain locations in the room. The students are not just stuck in their desks doing a worksheet. This is also a great way to use differentiated instruction. Students work at the circuits at their own pace. Here is how you can transform your normal worksheet into an engaging activity:

1. Divide your questions/activities into 4–6 stations.

2. Each station will have 3–4 duplicate copies with a question/activity written on it. Each station should be named a letter like A,B,C, and so on.

3. Make an answer station. This is where the students can go to check their work from the other stations. Maybe this is station E.

4. Spread out your station papers around the room. I try to have at least one or two stations on the floor. It is easy to put 3–4 desks together to be a station. The hallway is another possible location. The teacher's desk is always a favorite.

5. Have students write out the answer to each station on a piece of paper. They are asked to either show you when they are done, or actually turn it in. This creates accountability.

6. Encourage students to do the problems at their designated locations instead of moving problems back to their original seat.

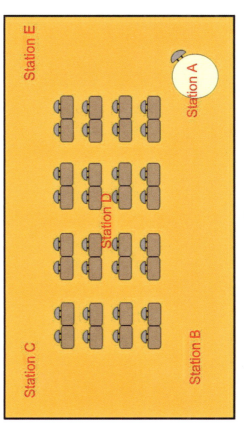

# Auditory Sentence Ordering

Most teachers are visual learners. If you are a visual learner, you usually present things visually. There are many students in your class that are auditory learners. These students are often ignored in our classes. Here is an activity that will address your auditory learners and help build auditory skills for the other students.

**Order these sounds**

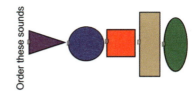

1. Find content that has 4–5 sequential steps in it. (The activity is very difficult with more than 5 steps in it.) Examples: the sentences in a paragraph, the steps to a math problem, or directions to an activity.

2. Make notebook-sized paper shapes that represent the sounds or sentences that you have made. Use colored paper to make it easier for students to discuss the activity with their partner. Tape the shapes to the front board in the room in a random order.

3. Make a written key for yourself associating each shape to a written word or sentence. You will use this when students pick a shape to "hear."

4. Randomly pick a student and his or her partner to come up to the board to select a shape to "hear."

5. If they pick the circle, then you look at your key and say the sentence that is associated with that shape. They might ask to hear it again. Give some time for the pair of students and the rest of the class to discuss with their partners where that shape belongs in the sequence.

6. Now have the pair of students reorder the shapes while justifying why they changed the order.

7. Repeat step 4–6 until all the shapes are heard and ordered.

## Easy Video Recorders

Easy Video Recorders help the students become the teacher. They are an excellent tool in the classroom because of their versatility. Students and teachers alike love them because they are so easy to use. Here is an example of how to use the video recorders in the classroom.

1. Randomly select 3–4 people for a group.

2. Give them a "problem" to explain. It could be a problem, scenario, ranking, or classification.

3. Give them a white board marker and eraser, a mini whiteboard, and a video recorder. Find simple video recorders that are easy to use and that don't cost a lot of money (iPads work great too).

4. Have them go into the hall or another room to work out the problem. The rest of the class will work on something else while these students are working on their video.

5. No face should be recorded. This helps the students feel safe and more comfortable making the video.

6. After each member introduces themselves, the problem should be stated in the beginning of the recording. The group members should take turns explaining the solution to the problem. Then the group should thank the audience for watching.

This process gives accountability to each member of the group. It deepens their understanding of the topic. They must know it because they have to TEACH it. Furthermore, students like to perform. When the group is done with the video, I give the "problem" to the rest of the class for some process time. Then I show the video to them. We sometimes need to clarify the group work. This is also a great way to create engagement with the other students when viewing the videos.

# Left-Right Talking (Structured Partner Work)

Get your students in pairs and sitting next to each other. Give a question for the students to think about in a short time frame. Opinion questions work really well with this activity. The person on the left gets to talk first. They will get a certain amount of uninterrupted time (15–60 seconds) to explain their solution or opinion. Now the right person will have a chance to reply to the "Left's" comments and may add their own as well for the same amount of time (15–60 seconds). Depending on the question, you might have another round of having the left and right talk.

This is a perfect time to randomly select students to report what THEIR PARTNER said. This creates accountability in the activity because students know they have to listen to their partner's position.

The activity gives power to the quiet student. Everyone will have a voice. Risk is lowered because each is reporting what someone else has said instead of what he or she said him or herself.

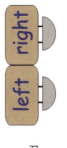

# Energizing Brain Breaks

Students are in their seats too much. Energizing Brain Breaks are a way to get students out of their seats and up and moving during the middle of class. I believe so much in Brain Breaks that I wrote a book with 50 activities called *Energizing Brain Breaks*. Energizing Brain Breaks are short 1–2 minute mind and body challenges. They help students to refocus. They should be done every 30 minutes. When a Brain Break crosses the midline of the body it helps both sides of the brain engage. They are simple to give with no preparation and no extra supplies.

The picture shows the "Ear and Nose Switch" Brain Break. You touch your nose with one hand and you grab your ear with the other. Then you try to switch back and forth as fast as you can.

# Take a STAND

Students love to give their opinion. Give them the opportunity to stand in the place where their opinion takes them.

4 Corner Stand: Have each corner represent some type of answer to a question. For example, "Which president would you rather be: Abraham Lincoln, George Washington, Thomas Jefferson, or John Adams?" Have the people in each corner discuss with each other why they are there. Then call a student at random from each corner to explain why they chose that answer.

Continuum Line Up: Have the students line up anywhere on the line from one answer to another. For example, "Which method of solving a quadratic do you like the best: algebraic or graphing?" Students can stand in the middle or at one side or another. Call on students at random for why they are standing at the place they chose.

# Invest in a Timer

**00:01:00**

**Start**  **Restart**

Get a countdown timer for your class. It is an excellent way to guide your students to use their time wisely. When a timer is used, there is a renewed sense of purpose. Most of all, a timer keeps us teachers accountable. We often tell our students they have 1 minute to finish. Then before you know it, 5 minutes have passed by. A timer keeps us accountable to all the students and shows that we need to either extend more time, or finish up the activity. It is nice to have a timer that all students can see. This can be accomplished if you have a data projector and an Internet connection. Just do an Internet search for online timers and you will find many possibilities. You can buy a handheld timer at a local store. These do not cost a lot of money. You can also work within the framework of your many software programs. They are usually built right in.

# Music During Assessments and Work Time

Students almost always have some type of noise in the background. It is rare when there is no sound at all. For this reason, I think it is important to avoid awkward silence by playing music without lyrics during assessments. It calms and eases the tension of the assessment for some students. It is also a great way to drown out the sniffle noises and any other sounds that distract students in the classroom when things are silent. Always tell your students a day in advance that you will be playing some music without words. Ask them to talk with you if they have any objections. I actually play classical music during my assessments. You can find some classical music playlists on the Internet very easily. Also you can ask your students to suggest styles of music and artists.

# Communicating With Your Students at Eye Level

When you put yourself on the same level as your students, you will find you have a better connection with them. Your communication is more collaborative than top-down. Students immediately are more relaxed when they see you at their level. A good way to do this is to use a rolling chair to move from student to student during work time. With a rolling chair this usually puts you next to your student. This sitting placement of side to side work is very positive. Typically you stand over a sitting student. When you are on a rolling chair you see your students at their level. Even if you don't have a rolling chair, you can sit next to a student with a chair instead of standing while helping them.

# Circular Teacher's Desk

If you have a chance to pick out the desk for your room, then pick a circular teacher's desk or circular work desk. Circular desks give the message to students that they can come up and get help. These desks are great for helping a group of students. Several students can gather around the table and see what is being done or hear what is being talked about.

Some circular desks can adjust to different heights. This is perfect in that you can sit with the students or you can stand with them.

I use my circular desk to help students in the morning or during any class work time. I adjust the desk to standing height so that students feel welcome to come up for help. It is very inviting for hesitant students. I also use it as a station in my circuit activities.

# Partner Desk Set-Up

Partner work is a great way to have students engaged in their work. Partners give students a way to communicate their learning. It also gives students a little security in doing their work. Below is how I would suggest setting up your desks. I personally use the triangular desks. They give a little bit more collaborative feel when working with their partner. Our district purchased desks that can be used as whiteboards.

**Rectangular Partner Desk Set-Up**

**Triangular Desks**

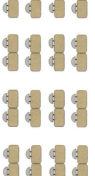

# Fidgety Students

Do you have any fidgety students? Why don't you give your students the opportunity to do something while they are learning? Fidgety students love to keep themselves moving. We can relieve this tension by giving them something to manipulate. I have found it successful to offer "things" for students to fidget with. I just put many of these things on a shelf for students to get them when they need them. My favorite is pipe cleaners. They are easy to manipulate, and they are cheap. Here are some other examples:

a. Koosh or Nerf ball
c. Rubber hand strengthener
d. Kneadable eraser
e. Silly Putty
f. Rubber band

53

# Personal Mini White Boards

Our school invested in a set of 30 dry erase boards for each classroom. They included dry erase pens and erasers. It paid dividends very quickly. The students love them. Here is how we use them. Each student is given a question. Then, the students work out the solution on the white board. They then circle their answer on the mini white board. I ask the students to hold up their white boards all at the same time. I can scan the room and see easily how many students are getting the problem correct. The students love it because they can discreetly give their answer.

This is just another way to get quick feedback for the teacher and student. It works out nicely because the students really own this activity.

ATTITUDE ADJUSTMENT

# Don't Complain…Teach Them!

I was complaining to the head basketball coach about my team not being able to play man-to-man defense. I did not get the sympathy I was looking for. He told me that I needed to teach them how to play man-to-man defense. It was a simple and profound statement that I have used over and over in my teaching. Now, when I start to think about how poor my students are performing, I NEED TO TEACH THEM. I need to find a way to get the material across in an effective way.

I am guilty of complaining about my students. I have stood in the teachers' office and said to my colleagues, "I told my students such and such SO MANY TIMES, and they still don't get it." Well, guess what? I need to find a way to engage and involve my students. I need to find a way to get through to more students. Then I need to remind myself that I got into this profession because I like to help my students. I want to make a difference. Here is my chance. Be Creative. Be a Problem Solver. Be a TEACHER and TEACH them!

# Name 13 Virtues of a Teacher

Ben Franklin gave us the 13 Virtues of a Person. I have taken that idea to a different level and am asking, "What are the 13 Virtues of a Teacher?" I think each one of us has a different opinion on this. Take this challenge and try to think of 13 virtues that you possess. Naming the 13 virtues will confront you with what is important to you and your teaching. Here are some words that some have used as their virtues: Acceptance, Adaptable, Attitude, Caring, Collaboration, Communication, Compassion, Consistency, Determination, Dignity, Discipline, Empathy, Explanation, Facilitate, Fairness, Forgiveness, Helpful, Hopeful, Humility, Humor, Integrity, Instruction, Intelligence, Kindness, Knowledge, Listener, Organization, Passionate, Patience, Professionalism, Questioning, Respectful, Trust, and Understanding.

Once you have completed the difficult task of narrowing them down to 13, take a virtue and think about it for the whole week. Try to use it daily throughout the week. Then move on to the next virtue.

## 20 Years Later

You make a difference! Your actions will last a lifetime for your students.

A colleague told me a story that has really made a big impression on me. He said a former student called him up out of the blue and asked him to meet for coffee. After catching up a little, the former student brought up an incident where my colleague had confronted him about cheating. The former student had denied it at the time. Now, over coffee, 20 years later, he confessed that he actually did cheat and it had been bugging him for years. Wow. Can you believe that?

I think this is a tribute to the teacher! This teacher must have made a difference in this student's life. There would be no reason to come back 20 years later unless he had made an impact on that student. Just think what your many students might think of YOU, 20 years later. This made me think that we as teachers are planting seeds in our students. We can only hope and pray that the seeds will continue to grow.

# Every Student Has a Story

We never know what our students are going through. It is important for us to *listen* to their stories. Here are a few ways to do that:

1. Establish a relationship. One way is to daily greet your students.

2. Tell your story. Tell of a difficult or rewarding experience you have had.

3. Ask your students to write the answers to these questions: What are the names and ages of your siblings? Describe one in detail. What are the names of your parents/guardians? Describe one in detail. Describe your current house/place including where you spend the most time.

4. Have monthly "check-ins" with your students. This could include talking about grades, attendance, and so on.

I have to remind myself that most students act out because of something in their life. This is why it is important to know their "story."

# Name Five Things You Are Grateful For

One of my more challenging classes in a long time was getting the best of me. My co-teacher and I decided to try to be grateful for the things they were doing instead of the things that they weren't doing. We decided to share five things that happened in class that we were grateful for at the end of every class period. The first day I couldn't find five. This was because I was still in the mindset of finding things that were wrong, instead of finding the things that were right. The second day we really started to look for positives. It was really powerful. I certainly struggled to get to 5. However, as the weeks passed, I found it easier to find five things that I really appreciated. Amazingly, I started sharing with the class some of the things that I was grateful for. Have you ever heard that you can't move a big rock unless you move it a little at first? Well, this turned out to be the movement of the rock. Try it with your students.

Be Thankful

# Reflect on Each One of Your Students

I call it prayer. You might call it meditation, reflection, thinking over or pondering. Whatever you call it, when you reflect on your students, you get invested in them. When we are invested in our students, then we do things for them that are in their best interest. I would encourage you to reflect on your students one by one outside of class. Think about them as people. Think of them 20 years down the road. Visualize them being successful. Think positively about them. It is really fun. It takes us as teachers to the place where we know they can go. You don't have to spend much time on each student; however, make sure you pause for each individual student. One way I do this is I take out my seating chart and pause at each name. You could also take a picture of your class and then look at each student when you are reflecting on them. Sometimes I just go through the class row by row trying to remember them.

# Power of the Parent

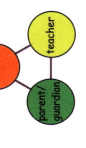

The parents/guardians of our students have a lot of power. Here are some suggestions for tapping into this power to help motivate and encourage our students.

- Open up communications early.
- Call all parents/guardians in the first few weeks of school.
- Give weekly updates.
- Make a contract with the student.
- Give a written note, an email, or a phone call update to the parent.
- Invite the parents/guardians to watch a class.
- Parents love to talk about their children. Create as many of these opportunities as you can.
- When parents are disgruntled, try to speak with wisdom and tact.
- Have the student be a part of any meeting or discussion.

# Open Parent/Guardian Communications Early

A phone call to the parent/guardian during the first couple weeks of school is ideal. This starts out the relationship on a great note. This phone call should be very short. The purpose is to "open" the relationship. Here are some things you will want to communicate to the parent/guardian in this initial phone call:

1. I'm excited for the start of the school year.
2. I want to get to know your child as fast as possible.
3. Please call or email with any concerns you have. The school phone number and email are on the website.
4. Is there anything that I should know about your child?
5. I would like to invite you to watch the class any time you would like.

# Invite Parents/Guardians to Visit the Class

*You're Invited*

Have you considered inviting parents/guardians to see your class in action? This simple act will build trust immediately. Give an invitation to any of your students' parents to visit your classroom while school is in session. Have them see what environment their child is in. You can have parents come in on a certain day, or you could set up individual times when they can come in. Sometimes parents are shy about coming because it might embarrass the student.

Upper grade teachers can give the invitation to visit a class other than their child's. Most parents/guardians will never take you up on the offer of coming to visit the class, but for the parents that actually come to class it will be an eye opening experience. Most parents have not seen the classroom for a long time. Their view of the classroom is the one that they grew up in. The current classroom is likely to be much different.

# Book Discussion Questions

**With a small group of fellow teachers, choose one of the 50 teacher tools (techniques) in this book to discuss. Read through it together. Then respond to the following together.**

1. Give one positive aspect of this technique.

2. Give one challenging aspect of this technique.

3. Do you presently implement this technique in class? If so, how?

4. Rate the technique on a scale of 1 to 10. Why did you answer this way?

5. Explain how you could modify this technique to work in your own classroom.

6. Where does this technique land on the issue of "time invested" compared to "results produced"?

7. How does this technique address the "engagement level" in your class?

# REFERENCES

Small, M., & Lin, A. (2010) *More Good Questions*. New York, NY: Teachers College Press.

Marzano, R. (2007) *The Art and Science of Teaching*. Alexandria, VA: Association for Supervision and Development of Curriculum.

Quinn, Pat.? Dupage Valley Math Conference, Dupage, IL.

Lemov, D. (2010) *Teach Like a Champion*. San Francisco, CA: John Wiley & Sons.

Kanold, T. (2011) *The Five Disciplines of PLC Leaders*. Bloomington, IN: Solution Tree.

Sladkey, D. (2009) *Energizing Brain Breaks*. Naperville, IL: Energizing Brain Breaks.

Burgett, J. (2007) *Teachers Change Lives 24/7*. Novato, CA: Jim Burgett.

Johnson, D., & Johnson T. (2008) *Joining Together: Group Theory and Group Skills*. Boston: Pearson.

Cantor, L., & Cantor M. (2001) *Parents on Your Side*. Bloomington, IN: Solution Tree.

# ACKNOWLEDGMENTS

My Wife, Linda: You are the BEST. Your wisdom and expertise is amazing. Thank you so much for many hours of editing and constant talk of "the book."

My Family: Thank you Kelly, Jamie, and Carl for your love and for supporting me in this project.

Naperville Central High School Math Department: It is a privilege to be working with such talented and dedicated people. Thank you for your daily commitment to excellence in teaching. You inspire me. Go Redhawks.

Naperville Central Colleagues: Thanks go out to Janet Kay, Vicki Michel, Scott Miller, Jackie Thornton, and Stephanie Vinton for your help creating the Engagement Wheel.

Editors: Beth Jasinski, Susie Johnson, Randy and Sue Pippen, Kelly Sladkey, and Linda Sladkey. Thanks for the wonderful job of editing.

My Past and Current Students: You are the true stars in this book. I love your energy and passion for learning. You make every day a wonderful adventure.

The Corwin logo—a raven striding across an open book—represents the union of courage and learning. Corwin is committed to improving education for all learners by publishing books and other professional development resources for those serving the field of PreK–12 education. By providing practical, hands-on materials, Corwin continues to carry out the promise of its motto: **"Helping Educators Do Their Work Better."**